vintage inspirations

# vintage inspirations

Jane Cassini & Ann Brownfield

photography by Caroline Arber

RYLAND
PETERS
& SMALL
LONDON  NEW YORK

*Designer* Sarah Walden
*Senior editor* Clare Double
*Senior designer* Sally Powell
*Location and picture research manager* Kate Brunt
*Location and picture researcher* Emily Westlake
*Production* Deborah Wehner
*Art director* Gabriella Le Grazie
*Publishing director* Alison Starling

*Text by* Jane Cassini
*Stylists* Jane Cassini and Ann Brownfield

First published in the United Kingdom in 2002
by Ryland Peters & Small
Kirkman House
12–14 Whitfield Street
London W1T 2RP

www.rylandpeters.com

10 9 8 7 6 5 4 3 2 1

ISBN 1 84172 286 3

A CIP record for this book is available from
the British Library

Printed and bound in China

# contents

# introduction

*Vintage Inspirations* reveals the beauty and surpassing charm of vintage objects, fabrics and ephemera, and shows how they can be adapted for the contemporary home. It tells you what materials to look for, where to find and how to use them. As you give your surroundings the individual stamp that only vintage can bring, you will develop a decorative style completely your own.

Vintage objects are intriguing – you might see a filigree brooch, a glass button or a length of braid, and as you contemplate the design, the colour, the shape and feel of a vintage item, you become part of its history. You wonder where it came from, imagine the people who once owned it. From an intricate piece of lace to a modest string of beads, the mystery and magic are indefinable, but undeniably there.

As this book shows, vintage objects can be displayed on their own or combined with modern materials to create a fusion that gives nostalgia a modern edge. Elegant, pretty, dramatic or subtle – any of these qualities will emerge depending on your selection, and how you use the materials you find. Whether it is for a special gift or celebration, a stylish collection or stunning accessory for the home, the charisma of vintage shines through.

It crosses boundaries, spans eras, transcends fashions. When the craftsmanship of the past meets the design ideas of today, the result is *Vintage Inspirations*.

**Opposite** Flowers made from delicate silk organza of old gold, mauve and palest pink evoke the era of the vintage corsage.

**Above left** A charming handmade notebook, embellished with fragile glass buttons set within a cut-out window, has a decorative handle of tiny gold and glass beads.

**Above right** A piece of Victorian silk, a twist of hat-veil and a necklace of copper beads – all pinned to a handwritten note – form an evocative collection of framed mementos.

*Dreams of vintage – captured in intricate lace, reflected in chandelier crystals, cultivated in pearls within flowers, woven in elegant embroidery – restore memories of things past to inspire ideas for the future.*

# inspiration

**Opposite** A pinboard is the perfect way to view work in progress – it can be constantly updated, and holds everything from fabric remnants to tantalizing bric-à-brac: anything that fascinates and intrigues. Deep shelves contain a variety of vintage 'finds', with hatboxes, bowls, vases, a filigree tray and a jardinière making interesting containers.

**Right** Spools of hat trims and ribbon.

**Far right** A length of unusual braid studded with diamanté. Behind it, buttons decorate the cover of a handmade sourcebook which contains scraps of vintage materials.

**Below** A spray of metal oak leaves and hat trimmings entwined around a jardinière.

# gathering

The dictionary defines vintage as 'of high quality, especially from the past', and so vintage objects are of a certain age and style. If you find yourself gazing at a Venetian glass necklace, or a lustrous silver tassel, or silk velvet ribbon, you could soon find your passing interest developing into a grand passion for all things vintage. Cast your net wide – with each new find, your collection will take shape, and your own style will evolve. How should you display your finds? A corner with deep shelving and a pinboard enables you to gather them within a changing display, ready to inspire ideas and to be reused in original ways. Here, a spool of silk ribbon and a sensuous pile of satins are a source of visual pleasure while they await a new role. A card of French buttons has already been cast as an *objet trouvé* in a picture frame.

This page Victorian and twentieth-
century lace, and cards with lace
trims; over an iron bed, a wedding
dress with overskirts of embroidered
net, and silk flowers at the waist.

A checklist of vintage items to gather and collect would include
beautiful buttons and buckles, sparkling diamanté, spools of thread, silk
flowers, remnants of fabric, ribbons and braid, old keys, tassels and
trims, crystals from chandeliers, songsheets, manuscripts, faded
photographs, feathers, illustrations…and ephemera such as postcards,
labels, tickets and theatre programmes. There are still plenty of these
vintage items to be found, so get gathering!

Victorian and Edwardian lace is still commonly available, and even
twentieth-century machine-embroidered net has charm. Be inspired
by the lace displays in antique shops and use the ideas at home, piling
it high on cut-metal trays, in wire jardinières and woven baskets.
Pieces of vintage clothing, with their intricate designs and beautiful
detailing, remind you of the exquisite workmanship of the past,
deepening your appreciation and fuelling your passion for vintage.

*Gather elements from another era – luxurious lace, glamorous diamanté, opulent embroidery – and begin an exciting journey of discovery.*

**This page** A wrought-iron chair makes a dramatic backdrop for a stunning black velvet and ivory satin embroidered evening dress and a crêpe de Chine blouse with a trim of diamanté and seed pearls. Both pieces evoke the glamorous era of the 1930s. The embroidery and beading found in vintage clothes of the 1920s, 1930s and 1940s often feature workmanship of exceptional beauty and quality. Whether you buy such garments in perfect condition to wear, or to make into an arresting display, they are a wonderful source of inspiration. Any pieces that are damaged or torn should also be rescued – they can be unpicked, and the salvaged beading, buttons and trims kept for reuse.

Far left The past is reflected in a mirror and comes full circle in this timeless second-hand clothes shop. A tailor's dummy displays a 1930s dress of sumptuous quality and exquisite workmanship.

Left Outside the same shop in a city alley: a jardinière piled high with beautiful lace, and a basket of silk flowers.

Below A silk handkerchief holder and a pile of satin and crêpe de Chine, waiting to be rediscovered.

# sources

To create your own vintage style you must first assemble the ingredients. Where are they to be found? Sources of affordable treasures abound. They include antique markets, collectors' fairs, charity shops, antique emporia, market and bric-à-brac stalls, car-boot sales and auctions. In a junk shop or antiquarian bookshop you could find a fascinating photograph album or a shoebox full of amazing picture postcards. An old-fashioned haberdasher's might still have a stock of trims and accessories. A second-hand clothes shop might yield fabrics from the past with intriguing names – cretonne, batiste, georgette, holland, sateen or spangled chiffon. One of the beauties of vintage is

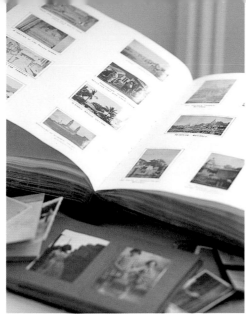

that whatever your style – elegant, exotic or eccentric – you will find something that reflects it, so follow your own taste. It won't be long before you start recognizing the possibilities inherent in any piece. Fragments of grandeur should not be missed, nor the most modest trifles. Seen with the eye of the vintage enthusiast – who imagines things in creative and decorative contexts – any interesting object, complete or dismantled, scratched or damaged, has potential. Your search will be enthralling.

**Left** Period photograph albums give an evocative visual record of the past.

**Below left** A fragment from a grand chandelier, with its superb crystal pendants, is a fascinating find. Even a single pendant can make a beautiful decoration.

**Below** A metal wreath and pair of wrought-iron nineteenth-century plant-pot stands spill out from an antique shop resplendent with chandeliers, candlesticks and mirrors.

*Intricate metalwork, a gilt mesh purse, porcelain roses – sources of inspiration from another age.*

Far left and inset A wooden jardinière is festooned with a fantastically ornate French nineteenth-century painted metal wreath made up of garlands of leaves, ferns and enamelled flowers.

Below A beautiful hand-painted porcelain rose on a stem of gilded metal with oak leaves, formerly part of a garland. It is worth collecting broken fragments, especially when they are as lovely as this. They give inspiration, and can be incorporated into other vintage compositions or simply displayed on their own.

When browsing, you might come across whole shops or stalls full of intriguing items, so train your eye to isolate separate pieces and imagine how they could be used once you get them home. Nature has traditionally been a source of creative ideas and has inspired countless exquisite objects. Let it be your inspiration too – delicate skeleton leaves can be dipped in plaster or an oak leaf or seed-head painted gold. While exploring in shops and markets you are not just looking for things to buy; you are also looking at the wonderful designs, colours, textures and patinas of vintage materials – and as a result your own source of inspiration and ideas is enriched.

Those all-important chance discoveries are often made where you least expect them – a long-forgotten evening bag in the attic, a wire basket in a friend's garden shed, a tin box in a jumble sale. On a specific search, you will find wonderful clothing and accessories in vintage clothes shops, where the owners might be expert in their field and happy to share their knowledge with you. At collectors' fairs, where there is a concentration of beautiful material, you will glean all manner of fascinating information along with your finds. There is something of interest virtually everywhere. Remember it is the combination of different eras, fashions and styles, and the effortless mix of things that mysteriously seem to go together, that make vintage work.

**Above** In a London vintage clothes shop, pearl necklaces, powder compacts, brooches and buckles surround a fine collection of vintage bags from the 1920s, 1930s and 1940s. The bags are in different materials: woven tapestry, embroidery, sequins, satin and diamanté mesh. Some have gilt chain handles.

**Right** A 1930s French circular diamanté purse with gilt clasp, in pristine condition, epitomizes the high-quality workmanship of the time. This beautiful bag was probably crafted in Paris.

Clothing from the past provides a limitless source of possibilities for the home. Because vintage style is about recycling and reusing things in unexpected ways, it is worth looking at second-hand clothes which are torn or which at first sight seem unsuitable. They might contain beautiful trims or buttons that can be unpicked and used to decorate table linen; the fabric, cut up, could become part of a fabulous cushion; a piece of brocade might be turned into a drawstring bag. Moreover, vintage materials look sensational combined with modern fabrics, so even remnants or small pieces are worth salvaging.

**Above and far right** The ravishing window display of this London antique clothes shop features a fabulous array of vintage clothes and handbags. On an original 1940s shop-window tailor's dummy, or form, is an American 1950s Orlon beaded cardigan, still in beautiful condition. Cardigans like this will always be popular – the delicate beading can vary enormously from designs of spare, simple elegance to more intricate patterns covering the entire front. It is always worth looking out for damaged garments, which can be quite inexpensive, in order to salvage the beads and buttons, linings and wool. Just inside the window (above) is a selection of Perspex handbags typical of the 1950s.

**Above** Among a display of white linen nightdresses is a beautiful Victorian cream hand-crocheted shawl draped over a tailor's dummy. Remember to keep a lookout for remnants of lace to reuse.

**Right** Still in its original box is a 1920s French beaded clutch bag. For the true collector, it is always highly desirable to find accessories in their original packaging, as this adds to their value and usually means they will be in better condition. Beading like this can be inspirational – you could even make your own silk bag, perhaps in a much simpler way but still emulating the subtle colours and flower shapes of the original piece.

**Below** A Victorian cotton and lace camisole is displayed outside a vintage dress stall.

*Sublime tastes of the past conspire with those of the new – the glamour of vintage, at once simple and sumptuous, was born to intrigue.*

There is poignancy in contemplating something which is beautifully made. You might imagine the person who crafted it, or picture the person who once owned and treasured it. An evening purse still containing a partly completed dance card with its accompanying tiny pencil reverberates with associations and meaning. In a sense, by rescuing old things you become a recycler of human history. Sourcing vintage items is about translating the dreams and desires of another age into the present – and enjoying yourself in the process.

**Right** Splendid upholstery tassels of metallic or linen thread, along with some beautiful embroidered braids, were found in a street market and have many uses.

**Far right** A jumble of subtly hued industrial threads on original spools.

**Below** A soft fold of intricate lace.

# discoveries

All that glitters is a potentially useful vintage discovery – a diamanté buckle, for example, is charming, affordable and versatile. But look beyond jewellery to less obvious things of the past (a spool of thread, a glass gilded button, a tassel); and beyond fashion itself to ephemera (postcards, music manuscripts, labels). A vintage discovery might not be of great monetary value but, once found and used with ingenuity, it can be transfigured into a thing of beauty. An ornate tassel from an epaulette, glass crystal beads from a broken necklace, a length of braid with detailed tooling – all can be reused in imaginative ways. Sometimes you will know at once how they are to be used, and other times the elegant context might have to await a serendipitous later discovery.

**Right** As this eclectic mix of brooches, clasps, bracelets and necklaces shows, diamanté costume jewellery comes in an astonishing range of styles. With starbursts, arcs, circles and other geometric structures, these 'fantasy' jewels emerged in the late 1920s, in the spirit of Art Deco style. Within the reach of everyone, and suddenly in vogue, they defined an entire period. A nineteenth-century paste clasp, also made of glass, glows more subtly. Both paste and diamanté jewellery are essential vintage decorations.

**Below** Tiny buttons and beads are stored in a row of patisserie tins. In the background is an original hand-lettered sample card of miniature glass beads and buttons.

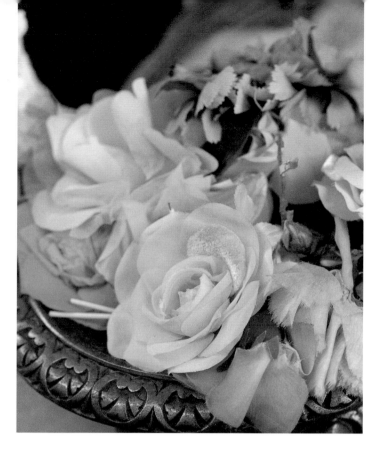

**Opposite above left** Beautiful glass 'Bimini' buttons with their gold lustre were made in London in the 1940s and 1950s. They were designed by an Austrian who lived in England and who is said to have been inspired by the shapes of some pebbles he found on the islands of Bimini, in the Bahamas.

**Opposite above right** Still on their original backing card are triangular mother-of-pearl dress buttons, probably of English origin.

**Opposite below left** A mixture of pearl and shell dress and coat buttons, some from Brazil, made between the 1930s and 1950s. Among the most beautiful of natural materials, pearl is drilled from seashells and freshwater shells from all over the world.

**Opposite below right** A selection of pressed-glass buttons from the 1920s and 1930s, and some cut-glass buttons on backing cards.

**Left** Silk millinery flowers from the 1930s and 1940s.

**Below** Victorian and twentieth-century lace trims in ivory and ecru.

Vintage inspires you to develop your own decorative style through discovering and reusing objects and fragments in new ways. Trust your instincts: through the process of discovery and selection, a personal style will emerge. As Cecil Beaton wrote, 'Only the individual taste in the end can truly create style or fashion.' If you turn a fragment of lace into a desirable gift bag, or a silk flower into a framed *objet trouvé*, your ideas are expressed and the charm of the object revealed. Beaton again: 'The beauty of these things is somehow transmitted through the personality of the one who chooses. It is in our selection, after all, that we betray our deepest selves, and the individualist can make us see the objects of his choice with new eyes.' By rediscovering vintage things, you extend their life and enable their inherent beauty to live on. 'Without mystery,' wrote Beaton, 'magic disappears.' In vintage, the element of mystery is ever-present. Where and when was it made? Who wore it? Vintage objects have a multi-layered magic.

The design qualities of vintage objects and materials, and the manufacturing processes that made them, have passed into history, so in a real sense you are involved in a race against time. Each discovery is an act of rescue, of salvage. The sense of the unexpected, and the knowledge that something, somewhere, is waiting to be discovered, sustains the feeling of excitement. You do not always need to be out 'buying'. In your own home you will discover useful vintage items — a brooch from an aunt at the back of a drawer, or a clasp on a dress in the attic. Take time, and look at details. Your own history is important: there are rich discoveries to be made in a hoard of old photographs, or your relatives might have some unwanted mementos that you could use. What makes your vintage discoveries come alive is using them in a new context and combining them in original ways. Their inherent artistry inspires you to dream up your own decorative ideas — a cut-glass brooch adorns a cushion, a sepia photograph features in a collage, intertwined necklaces become a tie-back for a curtain, an earring embellishes a fragment of mirror. And, in breathing new life into vintage materials, you create a link between past discoveries and present style.

**Above** An ornate Art Deco dress buckle with its ivy leaf and grape motif is surrounded by a stunning selection of Victorian and early twentieth-century buckles. These are all perfect for any decorative purpose. Even if they are broken, for example if the central bar is missing, they will still come in useful for display or embellishing a mirror.

**Right** A glittering array of brooches includes two diamanté sprays typical of the 1950s. Such items can be picked up for a modest price, but have plenty of charm and make delightful decorations.

**Far right** A paste dress buckle gleams against a background of black and gold and a 1930s diamanté and mesh purse.

*There is magic in the serendipity of your vintage discoveries – with a little ingenuity, every find has decorative potential.*

**Above** Draped around the neck of an elegant Art Deco-style gold mannequin is a beautiful 1940s Czechoslovakian rhinestone necklace set in brass.

**Left** On the glass shelves of a jeweller's shop window lies a 1950s cluster brooch with glass droplets. It is made of smoky cut glass and sprinkled with gold-coloured stones that have a distinctive iridescent sparkle. It was probably worn on the lapel of a suit jacket.

# home

*There is tangible pleasure in using materials from the past. Imbued with memory and meaning, they help define a style that is truly your own.*

This page Floral print, left; vintage necklaces of Venetian glass, pearls and plaited chains create a couture tie-back (if the necklaces don't join at the back, extend with wire or ribbon), below; an underskirt of ivory cotton tulle, dotted with faceted copper buttons, bottom.

Right A confection of three layers of material – bitter chocolate duchesse satin, a flash of mauve organza, ivory cotton tulle – makes a fabulous curtain. A floral print of mauves and smoky greys, originally a 1950s dress, is made into a seat cover and cushion for a 1940s chair.

# soft furnishings

Remember the time of summer frocks and satin ballgowns, pretty scarves and starched handkerchiefs, flirty hats and the *essential* piece of jewellery…

The era of dressing up returns to your home, creating an understated glamour. The grandeur of a ballgown is reinterpreted in a billowing duchesse satin curtain with underskirts of tulle and organza, the 'waist' encircled with a tie-back formed from intertwined necklaces. Lovely afternoon frocks, too damaged or unsuitable to wear, are perfect for remodelling into cushions.

It is important to retain simplicity. Vintage style has an inherent beauty that needs space, so don't overclutter. In this way the spirit of vintage is enhanced. Creating an engaging mix of pieces that surprise yet go together, seeing potential in the plain and the ornate – this is all part of the pleasure of vintage style, which involves collecting and reusing objects and materials in unexpected, serendipitous ways. Stunning pieces of costume jewellery, originally worn to add emphasis to an outfit, now accent a velvet cushion, the cut glass contrasting with the soft velvet. Equally, a modest diamanté button makes a statement when used to fasten a cushion cover.

*A fusion of new velvets and vintage jewellery expresses the mood of the moment: nostalgia, modern-edged.*

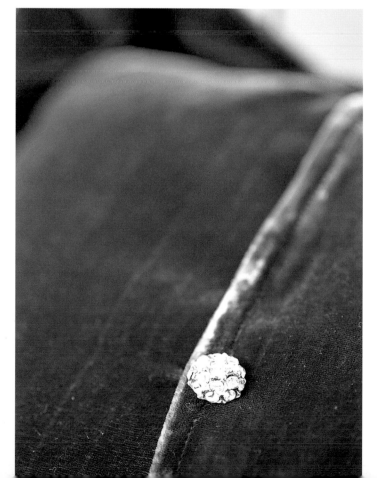

**Opposite** Distinctive pieces of costume jewellery have been chosen for their dramatic effect to accessorize a sumptuous pile of cushions. Pinned regally to each corner, glittering gems reflect the brilliant colours of the velvets, adding to the overall splendour.

**Left** Chic in its simplicity, a diamanté button provides a sparkling touch to the back of a velvet cushion cover.

**Above** A classic 1950s cluster brooch of golden-coloured and grey cut-glass stones, which would once have brightened the lapel of a simple tailored suit, now becomes the perfect adornment to a rich velvet cushion.

When pattern occurs in vintage materials, it is quirky, unexpected, beautiful. Vintage fabric patterns are often idiosyncratic, so they seem to recall a time when the artistry of the designer, or the skill of the embroiderer, still shone through. They retain an individuality which grows more enchanting with time. Look at fabric prints – delicate flowers of the 1940s, brazen florals of the 1950s, geometric inventions of the 1960s, psychedelic swirls of the 1970s – and you will see a whole era mirrored there. In your search for vintage materials, keep a lookout for scarves, remnants of fabric and pieces of clothing, and imagine how they might be used, on their own or combined with other fabrics.

When you come across a label inside an old garment, take a closer look. Usually machine-embroidered, often with immaculate stitching showing the name and even address of the design house, labels are time capsules from the past. Unpick them with care – not only are they fascinating in themselves, but they are valuable items that can be used in other contexts, for example on cushions, either singly or in rows.

**Opposite above** The geometric design of a chiffon scarf, loosely stitched to a velvet cushion, complements the lines of a 1950s Ernest Race steel and plywood Antelope chair. To one side, a small collection of other vintage scarves.

**Opposite below** A vintage dress label sewn onto a crisp linen cushion provides an intriguing detail.

**This page** Floral crêpe de Chine from an old tea dress, lilac silk and felted wool are pieced together to make cushion covers. A row of vintage dress and shirt labels decorates one panel.

*Against an ocean of white, dreamy eau de Nil, emerald and aquamarine bring memories of summers past.*

**Opposite** A cascade of pure white linen is caught at one side with casual elegance by a green spotted scarf. A café curtain ensures privacy and diffuses light onto a medley of chairs, each with its own vintage touch.

**Below** A green and cream 1960s jacquard scarf becomes a jaunty tie-back for the fresh linen curtain.

**Right** Embroidered and lace handkerchiefs, starched and hand-stitched together, make the prettiest café curtain. Choose only the finest linens and cottons, and keep all the handkerchiefs a similar size.

Rooms evolve as things are collected over time, and they change according to your mood or the season. One of the beauties of vintage style is its adaptability. Decorative ideas and colour schemes can emerge from a vintage item that holds memories or catches your eye – a faded green and white skirt, an aquamarine and citron headscarf. You might remember another pretty scarf or some embroidered handkerchiefs tucked away in a drawer. Vintage materials mixed with crisp new linen give memories a tangible place in your home, and nostalgia a contemporary slant.

*Yesterday's fashions – a summer skirt and a rose-patterned scarf – become today's home accessories.*

**Opposite** Cushion covers, made from an emerald and white summer skirt, hold memories of the Parisian street market where the skirt was found. The last sailboat button salvaged from a childhood sundress finds safe harbour as a fastener for the cushion cover.

**This page** Panels of floral fabric from a vintage scarf and new aquamarine linen are stitched together to make a chair-back cover – a simple way to unify an informal collection of chairs.

**Opposite above** Silk chiffon scarves of mauve, lilac and cream form a softly ruched overlay when wrapped around a lampshade. Catch with a stitch where necessary.

**Opposite below left** A raffia hat with a grosgrain bow is sewn to a miniature lampshade, and a silk tulle veil is added beneath to hide the fitting.

**Opposite below right** Vintage hat-straw has been steamed and stiffened into a traditional shape and trimmed with an unusual flowered braid studded with diamanté. To make the shade, an existing lampshade was removed from its frame to act as a template. The straw was cut and coated with liquid stiffener. When dry, it was steam-ironed flat, folded into a cone shape, stitched, hemmed, attached to the wire frame, then decorated.

*Witty, flirty, frivolous shades of temptation – see vintage in a completely new light.*

**Left** Part of an Edwardian organza and silk petticoat is gathered and attached to a length of petersham ribbon, then secured over an existing shade to create a romantic billowing effect.

Once you see how vintage fashion can be put to novel use in decorative lighting, you may never need to buy a mass-produced lampshade again. It is the immaculate detail that makes the difference. The picot edging of an Edwardian petticoat, the tailored bow of a 1950s hat, the sprinkling of diamanté on a flowered braid, the rolled edge of a chiffon scarf – all possess a quality and charm that shine through, and make light of your 'work', which is to rediscover and reuse them in original ways. So, loosely gather part of a silk petticoat, fashion a piece of hat-straw into a cone and edge with matching trim, use a hat with a bow, or enfold an existing shade in ice-cream-coloured silk chiffon scarves. Echoing the elegance of the shades, heavy Italian engraved glass stands (circa 1930–1950) add a final translucent touch. These are just a handful of possibilities. As your awareness of the potential of vintage grows, and you discover more and more useful materials, you will begin to come up with plenty of ideas of your own.

**Above** A simple wreath formed from dried long-stemmed flowers, bent around and secured with wire. Oak leaves are added and the wreath is then painted in gold.

# decorating walls

**Dramatize walls and mantels with stylized wreaths, beautifully framed *objets trouvés* and magical bejewelled mirrors.**

**Opposite** Skeleton leaves and seed-heads are wired to twigs bent in a wreath shape. Submerge in artists' plaster, remove, then leave to dry.

**Above** Photocopied book pages, cut into leaf shapes, are attached to a wire frame. Each leaf consists of two identical shapes folded lengthwise and glued together with a piece of jeweller's wire down the leaf fold. Leave enough excess wire to attach to the frame.

Usually associated with special occasions, wreaths can be a permanent form of decoration in their own right. Ideas can be gathered from intricate plasterwork, heroic laurel leaves, gilding, and from nature itself. Leaves and berries, twigs and seed-heads are transfigured into ornate plaster sculptures or gleaming gold metalwork when dipped in artists' plaster or coated with gilding paint. A distinctive paper wreath can be formed from the photocopied pages of an old novel. Ethereal or sculptural, these wreaths reflect the past and capture the spirit of today, enhancing any wall surface, distressed or plain.

**Opposite main picture** Mounted on ivory card in a frame of subtle charm, an operetta manuscript, a French theatre programme, a handwritten verse, a faded photograph, a remnant of hat-veil and other poignant fragments form a collage of evocative items.

**Opposite details** A Victorian metal hairpin with a postcard dated 31–12–23; an engraving pinned with copper ribbon and a topaz filigree heart.

**This page** Framed *objets trouvés*: exuberant typography on a remnant of music manuscript, the frame draped with fragile strands of diamanté; a music programme; a 1930s hair comb decorated with ribbon and a gardenia of stiffened cotton.

*Dazzled by diamanté, enhanced with pearls, mirrors travel far beyond the functional, to provide sparkling counterpoint to any room.*

**Left** A pearl earring adorns a pocket mirror inside a favourite handbag.

**Opposite** Setting up a sequence of dazzling reflections, an earring is glued to etched glass from a Victorian photograph frame, and attached with fine strips of double-sided tape to a mirror. Beside it, a smaller mirror is decorated with a pin of glass droplets. Both mirrors are embellished with braid.

**Details** The pin looks elegant on a small mirror; an earring, signed 'Robert', sparkles on the etched glass.

By finding and collecting interesting elements or fragments – a page from an old manuscript, a faded photograph, a lover's note, a ribbon, a brooch – you can create an evocative personal collage which exudes an understated beauty. Sympathetically framed, it can become a piece of decorative art. Search for things that are visually arresting, or that you find endearing, mysterious, fascinating. The collage is then a reflection of your memories and ideas; it expresses your taste, your daydreams, what you find moving. Even a single object, isolated and framed, can attain a dramatic beauty.

Mirrors reflect light, create space, and draw attention to a chosen feature. With pearls, crystals and diamanté, they become sparkling additions to the home and, once decorated, can be displayed singly or in a group. Where to begin? With the earring that has lost its companion, or the broken brooch that you cannot bring yourself to throw away, perhaps. So riffle through your jewellery boxes, browse around local markets, look for anything that gleams or reflects light. The older the mirror, the better the patina. If necessary, liberate it from an ugly or damaged frame.

**Opposite** Small oblong pieces cut from a broken mirror are dressed with diamanté buckles and brooches salvaged from a bric-à-brac stall.

**Above** A quartet of decorated mirrors is mounted on card using double-sided tape.

**Right and below** Displayed on a filigree picture-stand, a mirror created from a larger piece of damaged mirror, embellished with an etched glass photograph frame and a pearl drop earring. Double-sided carpet tape secures the photo frame to the mirror, and the earring is glued on.

A glazier will cut a damaged mirror into smaller, equal-sized pieces, which can be decorated and displayed in sequence. Alternatively, an unprepossessing mirror can be given an 'antique' bevelled edge to give it more form. If etched glass removed from the front of a Victorian photograph frame is attached to a piece of mirror, an extra dimension emerges, reflecting and enhancing anything you enclose within it, such as a radiant jewel.

# table decorations

Try a combination of crisp new linens and vintage trims and tassels, buttons and braids, to bring a sense of occasion to the dining table. With different shades, you can create a warm – or cool – sophistication.

From the fashion designs of Fortuny, Patou and Chanel to the Scottish kilt and the English 'uniform' of pleated skirt, twinset and pearls, pleating and braiding have long featured in fashion and influenced the way we dress. Bring a dash of couture to the dining table with pleated table runners decorated with vintage braids and tassels. Matching napkins and accessories such as a gorgeous bon-bon box, or personalized painted china, help achieve an inviting, intimate style that will charm your guests.

Mocha dominates the colour scheme in this table setting, where soft candlelight is reflected in antique French gold-inlaid glass, and table linen is highlighted with metallic gold braid and intricate tassels of finely crafted detail. Centre stage is an ornately decorated box softly lined with silk tulle and filled with golden dragées.

**Opposite and left** A heavy linen table runner with a pleated, decorated edge forms a dramatic backdrop to a romantic table set with gold-inlaid liqueur glasses and champagne coupe and a beautiful decorated box. The basic runner is a length of self-backed linen with the pleated edge made from a single, separate piece of linen. A length of rich metallic vintage braid hides the seam, with luxurious gold tassels and a tiny copper button providing a final flourish.

**Above** Chocolate-coated almonds, dusted with cocoa powder, are displayed in a *fin-de-siècle* champagne coupe.

**Right** Squares of linen are hemmed to make napkins, each with a faceted copper button at one corner.

**Opposite** A round box is covered with gold polyester 'paper', used by dress manufacturers and theatrical costumiers. The pleated edges are formed as the paper is pinched, folded and glued. The lid is decorated with a finely crocheted doily crowned with a silk and wire flower and a flamboyant tassel, and the box loosely lined with silk tulle.

When visiting market stalls, always keep an eye open for vintage braids, buttons, tassels and trims. Their intricate detail and craftsmanship act as foils to the crispness of new linen, adding depth and texture. Trims of gold and silver, once used to grace religious vestments and military regalia, are made from fine gold and other metal threads. While they are likely to be tarnished, which only adds to their authenticity and appeal, other items will benefit from a polish and emerge renewed. With the idea of bringing romantic charm to an intimate setting, and with your colour theme in mind — in this

instance, mocha — look out for markings of gold and copper on antique wineglasses, plates, candlesticks and other dining accessories. These do not have to be matching — an eclectic mix is beguiling. From a simple twist of old gold ribbon round a candlestick to the ornate trims decorating a bon-bon box, the quintessence of vintage charm is captured. In this way — combining old with new, respecting the past but turning it into something fresh and modern — an utterly individual style is achieved.

*Rich mocha and burnished gold evoke an intimate ambience and the candlelit world of the belle époque.*

**Opposite and below** A harmonious table setting shows the pleated edge of the runner with its vintage trims, draped gracefully over the side of the table.

**Right** A leaf and curling frond decorate a plain white plate. Use a porcelain and ceramic paint, following the manufacturer's instructions. Hand wash only.

Colour has the power to transform a look, so the simple act of changing table linens and accessories from mocha and gold to ivory and silver brings a total mood change — from warm winter intimacy to cool summer sophistication. Forming the focal point for a dining table is an ivory linen runner ending in a procession of pleats. The cotton gimp (or braid) which decorates the pleated edge is accented with cream linen tassels held in place by a striking diamond-shaped mother-of-pearl button. Plain white china can be given an individual touch by adding a hand-painted initial or leaf to each plate. Historically, the leaf is a recurring decorative motif, and initials were used by royalty and the aristocracy to personalize their china and commemorate important events.

*Cool ivories and milky whites, lit by iridescent mother-of-pearl and silver, lend an air of insouciance to summer dining.*

By adapting vintage materials and creating new contexts in which to see and use them, you are reinterpreting the past and putting a personal stamp not only on the objects themselves but on your surroundings. With vintage 'finds', it often happens that, rather than the decorative idea presenting itself first, it is the found object that gives rise to an idea about how or in what manner to use it. Thus it was with these trims and upholstery rings – first they were discovered in a remnant tray on a market stall, then later they inspired a use in a table setting. With this enticing mix of old and new, vintage treasures are transformed into stylish, contemporary additions to the home.

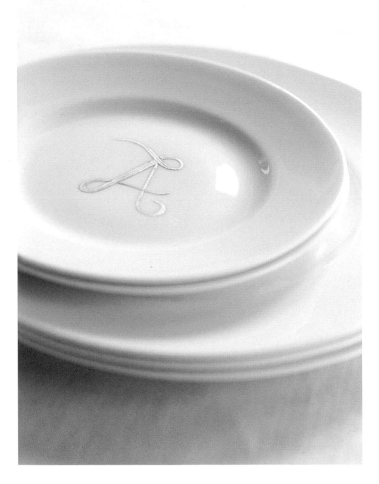

**Right and above** Ivory napkins made from squares of linen are folded and held in place by vintage cotton upholstery trims, which fasten like the belt of a raincoat. These pristine 1940s upholstery rings, perfectly matching the woven gimp, were discovered in a street market in their original unopened haberdasher's packet.

**Left** A bold, swirling silver initial is hand-painted on a white plate.

# plants and flowers

The appeal of silk organza flowers, fresh blooms or a simple bunch of herbs is heightened by the subtle addition of pearls, jewels and beads – delicate vintage dressing which extends into the garden with sepia or scripted labels and unusual planters.

Artificial flowers have long played a supporting role in fashion – from the modest sprays used for hat decoration in the nineteenth century to Madeleine Vionnet's magnificent chiffon rose ombrée of the 1930s, right up to the fantasy creations of today's couture designers, which signify, perhaps, a yearning for more romantic times. A corsage of fresh or fabric flowers typifies a time of elegance, when the smallest detail was all-important. With some effort and imagination you can create your own, in vintage style. Translucent silk organza is ideal for the petals, while lustrous pearls give the stamens a touch of splendour. Alternatively, a real rose is enhanced when highlighted by a vintage glass button. Whether you are making a glorious corsage or a simple display, the aim is not to reproduce the real, but to capture the essence.

**Centre** To create an artificial flower, make a stem by covering wire with double-sided tape. Bind with ribbon. Cut the petals from organza. Pinch each petal at its base, and glue one by one to the stem to form the bloom. Make a calyx from organza-covered card, and position at the flower's base. Stamens are made by wrapping tissue paper around wire, then adding a loop of pearls.

**Above** An organza corsage.

**Left** Ribbon-tied organza flowers in a slender vase.

**Far left** A 1920s mirrored button on one petal makes a rose into a fresh corsage.

*A wild way to wrap a bouquet – with hessian and seagrass, root tendrils and vintage jewels.*

**Opposite** The beautiful white blooms of (front to back) double lisianthus, calla lilies and trachelium are swathed in hessian, tied with seagrass or root tendrils, and decorated with special pieces of vintage jewellery.

**This page** Tendrils of entwined dried root conceal a topaz pin, above left; a 1960s brushed gilt bracelet with emerald green cut-glass stones encircles the hessian, right; a knot of seagrass is complemented by a brooch of diamanté set in a fine metal 'trellis', below left.

A stunning contrast of colour and texture is created when the exquisite forms of fresh white flowers are framed in swathes of rough hessian or linen and secured with decorative ties of plaited seagrass or dark root tendrils. Scattered hints of topaz, emerald and diamond reveal the discreet charm of the vintage jewel – a pinned brooch or an encircling bracelet. They bring a sense of the unexpected, and reinforce the element of contrast. If delicate pieces of jewellery are chosen, perhaps with intricate metalwork and small cut-glass stones, they will enhance, not overpower, the beauty of the fresh blooms. Bejewelled, swathed and tied – do the bouquets represent a personalized gift of flowers, or is this an imaginative way of presenting a piece of enchanting jewellery? They can be offered as both. They say it with flowers *and* with jewels.

**Opposite** A nostalgic scene: a hand-knitted garden drawstring bag, and a comfortable cushion with an embroidered vintage label sewn to one corner.

**Above left** Bundles of oregano, liquorice sticks and lavender, tightly bound with copper wire. The wire is threaded with glass beads of mauve and topaz.

**Above centre** Charming 1940s sepia photographs from a family album are photocopied and stuck on gift labels, which are tied to hand-sewn hessian sacks filled with bulbs.

**Above right** A wire planter becomes a grand outdoor vase for a voluptuous late summer display of snowberries, green timothy grass, birch twigs, oak leaves and china grass. Line a planter with moss, then conceal the container within.

**Left** A hand-lettered plant label provides an elegant touch to a lavender plant in a vintage Spanish tomato trug. A label holder is twisted into shape from galvanized wire brushed with copper paint.

# home work

**Paying bills, mending and doing the laundry feel less of a chore with vintage style incorporated into your work space in functional fashion.**

What could be more pertinent than books, manuscripts and print as inspiration for a practical work space? Illustrations, quotations, book bindings, manuscripts, typography – all provide an inexhaustible supply of available imagery. Title pages can be used as lining for storage boxes. Lines of poetry and quotations can be rolled into scrolls or made into hanging labels for personalized stationery. A fashion illustration, mounted on board, is transformed into a timepiece by attaching a clock mechanism. Candle boxes stamped with identifying numbers, their lids fastened with buttons, are stacked and used as storage containers. Apothecaries' canisters are recycled as pen and brush holders.

**Opposite** A profusion of items showing vintage at work.

**This page** A notepad made of old paper – the trim came from a roll of ribbon, top; a scroll of poetry tied with ribbon, above; paperweights made from seed-heads and berries dipped in artists' plaster, with a coil of wire decorating each stem, left.

**Right** With the addition of linen-thread loops and shirt buttons from the 1920s, candle boxes exchange their utilitarian looks for self-confident style. Sew the buttons on, or catch a few threads through the holes and glue.

**Below** An old book with a secret storage compartment cut inside is decorated with a length of narrow ribbon.

Books, files and ledgers can be covered in buff, cream or ivory paper, reminiscent of parchment and vellum, and then hand-lettered in gold along their spines. A secret compartment cut from the pages of an old book is perfect for housing drawing pins or paperclips, with the book cover forming the lid. Old wooden cutlery trays are worth salvaging – they provide useful extra storage for pens, rulers and office clutter. As an alternative to a shelf, a letter rack can be constructed out of plywood or MDF and painted a subtle colour. It will take up less room, can be propped or wall-hung, and will hold writing paper, envelopes and magazines in a coordinating display. For stationery, choose good-quality paper in fine shades: as well as creams and ivories, look at taupes, buffs and greys, and for interest add an accent colour, perhaps a mauve or lilac.

*All kinds of office paraphernalia can be housed in clever containers with a stamp of vintage detail.*

In these days of faxes and electronic mail, a handwritten letter is appreciated, especially if it is personalized by an apt quote or line of poetry. Search in second-hand bookshops for the captivating covers of old paperbacks, novellas, antiquarian books, 'penny editions', music manuscripts or songsheets – all represent a limitless source of decorative ideas. Adapt, change and put your discoveries to new use. With their distinctive craftsmanship and design, vintage finds have a way of retaining their original charm while adjusting extremely well to the modern world.

**Above** Music manuscript from the 1900s is photocopied onto tissue paper and pinned with a grey velvet rosette.

**Left** Title pages and songsheets are used to line old Basildon Bond stationery boxes, ideal for display and storage.

**Above** A pretty pincushion is hung on the back of a door near the sewing corner.

**Right** Elegant pincushions are made with new silks, trimmed with Victorian hat ribbon and embellished with brooches and diamantine pins. The pincushions are padded with kapok – in the past, sheep's wool, bran, iron filings or even coffee grounds were used.

Old books on needlecraft reveal the astonishing range of skills once considered necessary for an accomplished needlewoman. They included pattern cutting, dressmaking, crochet, embroidery, appliqué, tapestry, macramé and tatting, as well as basic mending and darning. Specific advice abounds for the budding seamstress: 'She should have a needlecase well stocked with a variety of ordinary needles – sharps and betweens – of different numbers. Then she should have a good supply of pins which may be kept in a small pin-box or cushion', advises one book from the 1930s.

Needlework items can still be found in bric-à-brac stalls and at collectors' fairs. You might find reels of linen thread, or tins with their original contents – needles, press studs, pins, hooks and eyes, buttons – all as useful now as they were then, and handy for sewing as well as craft projects.

**This page** A needlecase sewn from wool and lined with silk contains a pocket, a wool 'booklet' for pins (not seen), and stitched inserts of cotton tape. A 1930s diamanté button and a silver bullion loop provide the perfect fastening.

**Opposite** A quiet corner in which to sit and sew. The *Encyclopedia of Needlework* on the chair brims with excellent advice and is a pocket history of traditional skills.

**Right** A piece of brocade from the Edwardian era is lined with silk to make a bag. The drawstring is made by threading 1920s silk cord through Bakelite curtain rings.

Along with the useful advice in these old books is the acknowledgment that needlecraft is a creative and edifying activity – a notion that still applies today. So find a corner with a comfortable chair and, as a first step, for storing your tools, sew a few pretty needlework basics – a pincushion, a needlecase and a drawstring bag (also known as a Dorothy bag). You can achieve practical and charming results by using beautiful pieces of vintage fabric, trimming with old ribbons and upholstery cords, and combining them with contemporary materials such as soft wools and opalescent slub silks. Look for quiet and restful colours: oyster, ecru, old gold and greige – all suited to the contemplative nature of sewing by hand. Then there is the added pleasure of having a place to store your vintage sewing paraphernalia: quaint packets of needles, cards of darning threads, glass or mother-of-pearl buttons, spools of lustrous twist, wooden cotton reels, a silver thimble. As the *Encyclopedia of Needlecraft* points out, 'a practical knowledge of plain sewing enables one to appreciate other people's work at its true value'.

*Awash with vintage style – chic laundry accessories,*
*spotted and striped, in navy and white.*

In the 1920s, Chanel launched navy and white as the coolest colour combination, and it has remained a classic ever since. Spotted and striped navy and white fabrics give a pristine feel to the utility area. Headscarves and neckties are a good source, as are tickings, collarless shirts, rayons and crêpes de Chine from dresses and blouses. Incidentally, remember to retain the darts, buttons and bows from vintage clothing, as they can be incorporated elsewhere in decorative ways. After dry-cleaning, or hand-washing in gentle soapflakes, the fabrics are ready to emerge afresh as contemporary laundry accessories.

**Above** Linen slip covers for hangers have openings to take fragrant sprigs of lavender, with rayon ribbons attached for fastening.

**Left** Laundry bags fashioned from a 1940s striped blouse and a 1960s spotted scarf are backed with white linen, with neckties as drawstrings.

**Opposite** Navy and white bring a breath of fresh air to the utility area. A linen-covered box for toiletries is tied with a sash from a 1930s dress.

# dressing table

The mood is romantic as you dress for the evening – the story unfolds in silk satin and lace, and elegant accessories take a starring role.

A jewellery roll is a boudoir basic, protecting necklaces, rings and bracelets. A roll of silk satin overlaid with embroidered net and appliqués of rococo-style lace, fastened with ribbon and a dress buckle, is the ultimate in glamour. For later: a taffeta silk evening purse emblazoned with mirrored and gilded buttons. Fascinating fragments from the past – silk satin from a torn slip, a remnant of lace, a dress buckle, a handful of buttons – are reborn as today's vintage heirlooms.

**Opposite** A beautiful ensemble is softly reflected in the mercury mirror on a carved wood console.

**Right** An evening purse of taffeta silk, with 1920s buttons sewn in a cluster to form a bloom with a fragile stem of seed pearls.

**Below** A jewellery roll made of softly padded silk satin and overlaid with lace is fastened with ribbon slipped through a 1920s diamanté dress buckle.

# collections

The need to collect and display objects is deep
and instinctive. A faded photo, a postcard with
a special message, a memento from a romantic
holiday – such things hold memories and carry
emotional resonance and, presented imaginatively,
create a decorative personal record.

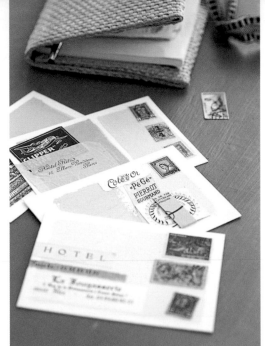

**Opposite** Vintage and contemporary materials combine to create handmade postcards, a straw bag and a raffia travel journal – all nostalgic holiday essentials conjuring up the leisurely past of straw picture-hats and folding cameras.

# mementos

Vintage ephemera such as tickets and postcards hold vanishing imagery. By being discovered and reused in new ways, they are transformed into lasting mementos, and their fragile beauty lives on.

**Above left** White card is painted with bands of colour, then overlaid with appealing ephemera to create unique handmade postcards.

**Far left** A notebook covered with modern raffia wall fabric and fastened with a striking hat ribbon becomes an original travel journal.

**Left** A bucket bag made from a circular piece of vintage hat-straw is painted with hat stiffener and steam-ironed into shape using a hat block to form the flat base. A 1920s silk upholstery cord is threaded through to form the strap.

Vivid memories of a holiday abroad – a favourite hotel, or café on the square – are etched into a few stamps, a menu card, a hotel letterhead, a twist of ribbon, a tissue wrapping. Transmitting their stored memories and associations, these mementos can be incorporated into handmade items – a raffia travel journal for notes and ephemera, or 'scrap-art' postcards. Edited and pieced together like amusing mini-collages, they become souvenirs to keep or send to friends.

**Left and below** A beautifully handwritten card from Venice dated 17.1.28. A page from the album displaying holiday keepsakes includes a chromolithographed postcard, an Italian hotel's luggage label, and a painted silk image of a flag.

*Postcards carry more than captivating images. Their stamps, postmarks and graceful pen-and-ink messages give beguiling clues to other times.*

Mementos and ephemera such as old postcards are saved for another generation when they are gathered and displayed in charming handmade albums. Fascinating and collectable, vintage postcards are redefined as art in an album setting. Covering an astonishing range of mood, subject matter and printing method – from evocative sepia photographs to splendid chromolithographs and enchanting watercolours – picture postcards first appeared in the 1870s. Collecting them became a favourite pastime when handwriting was still an art. There is a poetic link between these old postcards with their penned thoughts and the albums with their windows into past worlds of framed memories.

**Left and opposite** Albums made from folded sheets of watercolour paper are bound with faded vintage ribbon. The covers have cut-out windows, leading the eye in to postcards with exquisite calligraphy and an enchanting 1920s illustration.

*Black-and-white photographs, fixed with hatpins to an artist's canvas, become a mise en scène of images frozen in time.*

From images of fashion to graphic reportage, black-and-white photography epitomizes 'the caught moment'; with everything pared down to essentials, these images reveal the significance in the beautiful, the bizarre or the commonplace. An artist's canvas makes a theatrical backdrop for a collection of photographic images; touches of glamour are added by securing pictures with vintage hatpins or using plumes and faux flowers. Smaller canvases can be painted in blocks of colour, then decorated with a striking image and a corresponding brooch or clasp. Light-hearted and pretty, these canvases lend themselves to spontaneous additions and changes. They are a visual journal and a vision of an age, crisscrossing boundaries to form an exciting decorative focus.

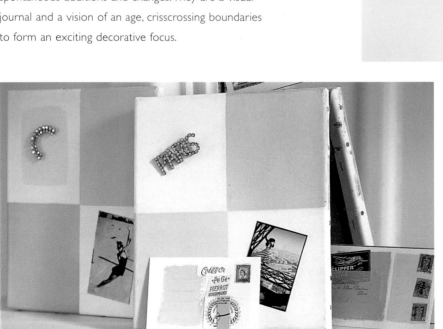

**Opposite** A glamorous scene in monochrome: a pinboard is dressed with iconographic and personal photographs, hatpins and faux flowers, while 1930s hatboxes with their idiosyncratic typography are stacked on a whimsical wire chair. The pinboard is a stretched canvas, backed with foamboard to secure the hatpins.

**Above** Vintage hatpins.

**Left** Small painted canvases hold a memorable black-and-white image and graphic piece of diamanté: a 1960s 'Paris' brooch, a 1920s crescent moon. Propped against them are the scrap-art postcards.

HILHOUSE & Co.
HATTERS
11, NEW BOND STREET, LONDON, W.1.

Lincoln Bennett "Hats"

**Opposite** Precious mementos are grouped on an artist's canvas painted in muted tones.

**This page** A family photograph is pinned to a signed note with a sprig of faux flowers, left; another is placed on a fragment of parchment edged with gilt braid and decorated with frayed metallic gold ribbon, above.

A treasure trove of mementos is beautifully framed within a grid of soft painted squares on an artist's canvas. The grouping of seemingly random elements – a photograph, an embroidered letter, a title page – creates a series of narratives, becoming at once a personal archive and an avant-garde display. The tone of the composition can be romantic or poignant, witty or humorous. Intuition and a discerning eye are needed to edit and assemble the ingredients, and to decide what to keep in and what to leave out. Moreover, the composition need never be finished but can change as the mood takes you.

A printer's type case, painted the same colour as the wall, seems to 'float', and the compartments lend themselves perfectly to the framing of vintage finds. Isolated, yet part of a composition, each object is seen afresh: a rusty key, a French picture hook, some poster type. Empty compartments give a sense of new discoveries to be made.

These cases housed metal type for letterpress printing. Cases with equal-sized compartments housed capital letters; these were placed at an upper angle, so the letters became known as 'upper-case'. Cases with different-sized compartments were kept at a lower, more accessible angle, for 'lower-case' letters, with the most commonly used in the larger compartments. When lithography replaced letterpress, type cases fell into disuse. Now they make apt showcases for vintage discoveries.

# treasures

Recapture the childlike pleasures of collecting, and arrange your vintage treasures in a new setting to reveal their distinctive character.

**This page** A white-painted type case against a pure white wall achieves a sculptural quality, emphasized by the intriguing mix of objects and deliberately bare spaces.

**Opposite** A French picture hook and accompanying bundle of nails, attached to the original backing card, left; poster type beside a Victorian buckle threaded with gold metal braid, right.

It is the links between the past associations of each treasure that give meaning. The inky sepia browns of the wood type 'blocks' contrast with the paleness of the freshly painted printer's case. Wood type, originally used in poster printing, can be coated with a gilding paint, and used to make gold-streaked impressions on small rectangles of rough art paper. The original ironmonger's mounting card for an embossed brass picture hook contains beautifully crafted typography which could easily be overlooked, but is brought forward in a stylish setting. Other items that have no connection with the printer's world are chosen for their connotations or visual qualities: a gleam of blunt silver or gold, perhaps, or an accent of diamanté.

A collection of imposing wood type can be transformed by paint into sculptural blocks of colour, giving a change of scale and a clean contemporary look. With its power to alter the way objects are perceived, paint brings out the designs of the typefaces in greater relief and, lined up on a shelf at random, or spelling out a word, they make a striking display.

**This page, top to bottom** In a printer's type case compartments: wood type, a diamanté buckle, a Victorian heart pin.

**Opposite above** Obsolete wooden poster type is reused decoratively.

**Opposite below** The gold-streaked imprint of a letter A pierced with a hatpin made from a glass Bimini button.

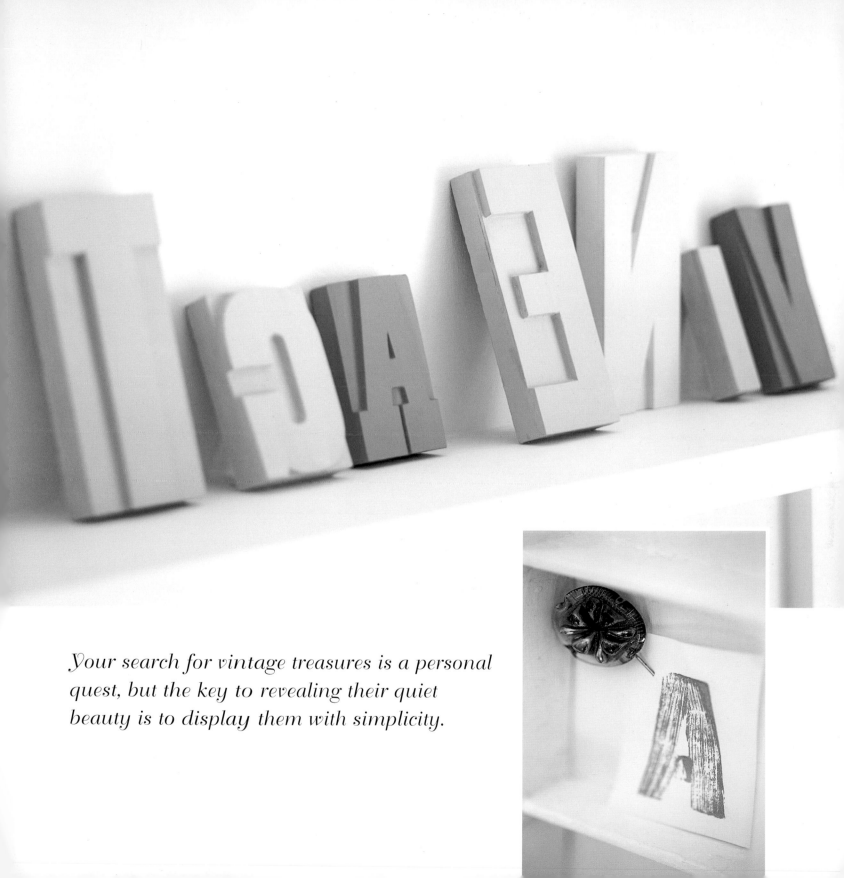

*Your search for vintage treasures is a personal quest, but the key to revealing their quiet beauty is to display them with simplicity.*

Fashioned from various materials, buttons incorporated the innovative skills of master craftsmen, and at one time they were valued not only as functional fasteners but as ornamental miniature works of art. Theatrical or refined, ornate or simple, the button is a collectable item.

*Vintage plastic, mother-of-pearl and pressed-glass buttons shimmer on the squares of a painted draughtboard.*

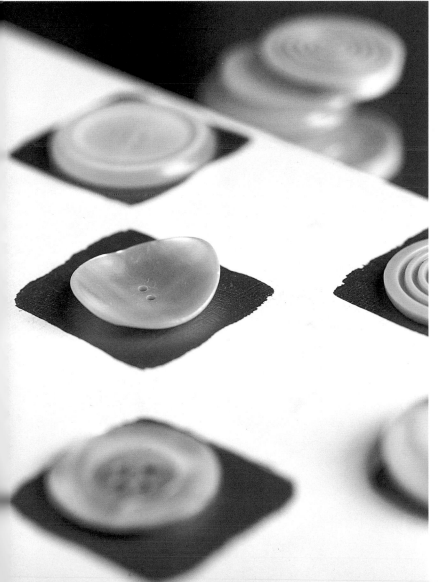

**Opposite and this page**
A delightful array of vintage mother-of-pearl, glass Bimini and plastic coat or jacket buttons find a new role as draughtsmen on a gold- and oyster-painted plywood board, making an attractive display.

Most family homes used to have a button box, where buttons salvaged from discarded clothes were kept. The childhood memory of playing with a button box was one inspiration for this idea of using buttons on a handmade painted draughtboard. The other was the chance discovery of some grooved moulded plastic buttons, probably from a 1940s coat, which were reminiscent of draughtsmen. Together with some opalescent vintage mother-of-pearl buttons, and Bimini buttons of hand-pressed glass with gold lustre detailing, they make a beautiful collection. The colours are subtly reflected in the gold and oyster squares, which were painted in loose brushstrokes on a cream background.

# celebrations

*This is where vintage becomes most fun –*
*where you can surprise and delight others,*
*while indulging your passion to the full.*

# wrapping gifts

A gift bag of vintage lace and velvet becomes a gift in itself,
and enhances the pleasure of giving and receiving.

Lace, that most romantic and evocative of textiles, first appeared in
Venice in the sixteenth century and was once considered more valuable
than gemstones. Exquisite wrapping makes the simplest of gifts alluring,
and these gift bags show the intricate beauty of this vintage material to
stunning effect. Yet they are so simple to make. Combine shades of cream
and *café au lait* lace, the palest of tissue papers, rich velvet ribbons and
the prettiest buckles you can find.

**Opposite and right** These translucent lace bags with supporting tissue lining were made as gift bags to hold fragrant soaps. To make a gift bag, cut out equal-sized rectangles of lace and tissue paper. With the tissue on top, fold in half and machine-stitch the sides. Then turn inside out to form a bag, folding part of the top inwards. Make a bow from a length of lace and hand-stitch to the bag. Thread a length of velvet ribbon through a buckle, and hand stitch to the centre of the bow.

**Below** Lustrous vintage ribbons threaded through a fascinating array of early moulded plastic dress buckles from the 1930s to 1950s.

# tea party

Relive childhood memories as you plan a children's tea party. Vintage picture books contain enchanting lettering for invitations, quixotic illustrations for decorating cards and crackers, and whole pages to twist into gift cones.

**Opposite** A children's tea-party table laid with party cones, decorative crackers and sweet bags. Muslin bunting trimmed with vintage tassels is festive.

**Above left** Crackers are formed from crêpe paper and tissue wrapped around a cardboard tube, the twisted ends secured with vintage braid. Photocopy handmade cards for decorative labels.

**Above right** Illustrate cards by tracing and painting, or photocopying, a favourite animal character. Ribbons are slotted though cuts in the paper to decorate the animal illustration and party envelopes.

Vintage comics and children's picture books – in any language – should be collected for their simple, colourful imagery, and the childhood memories they evoke. Cartoons and illustrations of animals – bears, rabbits, cats, and of course dogs, such as the fox terrier – are perennial favourites with children, and will always provide comforting inspiration for birthday cards, party invitations and crackers. The bold outline of an appealing animal can be photocopied, or traced and painted; and, for a jaunty touch, a strip of coloured ribbon can be tied around its neck, as if it is wearing a scarf or a lead. This can be matched with a ribbon slotted through the flap of the party envelope. Look for gaily coloured fabric remnants or old dresses in second-hand clothes shops – they are all useful for turning into ribbons and ties.

**This page** Sweet bags are made from tissue paper, folded in half and stitched. Make pretty ribbons from vintage fabric and knot each end.

**Opposite above** Ribbon decorates a hand-lettered nametag.

**Opposite below left** Party invitations are made from five label shapes. 'Invitation' is inscribed on the top card; name and address on the next couple; and time and place on the last two. Interleave with tissue paper cut to the same shape, and punch through for the ribbon.

**Opposite below right** Pages from an old Spanish lettering book are rolled into cones and secured with a spot of glue. Add an outer layer of tissue, twisting the end to form a seal.

*Set the scene, vintage style, with ribboned nametags and picture-book party cones.*

These days, no children's party would be complete without a party bag. One way to make party bags look fun and intriguing is to use original or photocopied pages from old comics and picture books. Roll them into cones, and fill them with little gifts. Another idea for writing invitations and nametags is to look at the quirky old-fashioned scripts in children's storybooks and copy their style. Sweet bags tied with ribbon add a tempting vintage touch to the table.

# the cocktail hour

A heady cocktail to instil a sparkling mood. Miniature fans,
silvered and gilded, balance in elegant coupes for champagne;
while fantasy masks, flirtatiously feathered, are adorned with
pendants of pearls and ties of silk ribbon.

Exotic Venetian masquerades and costume balls provide inspiration for an array of exquisite fans and teasing masks, which become sophisticated decorative accessories for a drinks party and tokens for the guests to keep. The translucent silver- and gold-striped tracing-paper fans – bound with fine embroidery bullion, and with a delicate hand-lettered name card suspended from each – personalize a collection of etched-glass champagne coupes, which are grouped in an empty picture frame to bring the arrangement into focus. The masks, made from gold and silver card, are adorned with marcasite and pearl pendants, gilt and diamanté jewellery, silk ribbons and swansdown feathers. Even the napkin rings are things of beauty – sewn from iridescent lilac silk, they are accented with sprays of sparkling diamanté.

**Opposite and below** Arranged on a console table is a pretty collection of vintage champagne glasses. Each has a pleated striped fan, which is personalized with a guest's name on a hand-lettered card. Party masks cut from gold or silver card, embellished with ribbons, feathers and jewels, add to the ambience.

**Left** These fans are created from rectangles of tracing paper striped with wax gilt, which is brushed between areas marked off with masking tape. Pleat into a concertina and bind at the base with bullion wire.
**Above** The napkin rings are lengths of lilac silk, folded and stitched, with diamanté brooches pinned at the centre.

# Christmas

With an evocative mélange of the simple and the ornate, vintage style comes into its own at Christmas. Shadowy greys and browns unite with icy white to enhance the seasonal magic.

Beautiful old Christmas cards are a good source of traditional, nostalgic images, and they can be photocopied to make festive decorations. Dress the tree in vintage finery – silver bullion tassels, luminous chandelier crystals, glistening costume jewellery, anything that sparkles intensifies the magic. Under the tree is a tumble of bejewelled parcels…and, on the mantelpiece, a fairy, on tiptoe, in anticipation of the special day.

**Above** This fairy, inspired by old-fashioned Dutch dolls, was made from modelling clay, painted, and dressed in silk tulle with tissue-paper overskirts flecked with silver and gold. The wings, tiara and corsage were formed by threading vintage beads onto fine wire.

**Left** Vintage tree decorations and real candles, lighted or not, impart a magical ambience. (Keep lighted candles away from other decorations and never leave them unattended.) The vintage theme is beautifully extended to gifts, which are wrapped in pleated tissue paper adorned with buckles, ribbon and jewellery, and to gift boxes, albums and crackers decorated with wintry images.

**Below** A piece of fringed bullion braid is coiled to form a tassel and stitched in place. The top is encircled with diamanté, and the hanging loop made from fine wire.

**Opposite right** A resplendent 1940s earring with starry clusters of diamanté and opaline stones is a perfect tree decoration.

**Opposite** Under the Christmas tree: a pile of presents is dressed with buckles and brooches, as well as pleats and vintage satin ribbon. Each gift box is carefully wrapped in tissue. Then a separate sheet, pleated lengthways, is laid around the parcel and secured in place at the back.

**Left and far left** A diamanté dress buckle; a starburst brooch of clear and amethyst cut-glass stones.

**Below** An old Austrian postcard is photocopied, mounted on card, and hand-lettered to form the album cover. Sheets of watercolour paper interlaced with glassine are folded in half to form the pages and the 'spine'. Thread ribbon through two punched holes at the side to secure cover and pages. Add a flat bow of matching ribbon.

A varied collection of dazzling diamanté will add glamour and glitz to Christmas gifts, enhancing the individual charm of each stylishly pleated, beribboned parcel. A mix of tissue papers in evocative shades of white, grey and brown echoes the seasonal colour theme. Sheets of white tissue can be flecked with silver and gold paint for an iridescent shimmer. Encircling each parcel, pale vintage satin ribbons are slipped through a beautiful buckle, or pinned with an elegant brooch to create irresistible 'fairytale' wrappings. And, to hold precious Christmas photographs, a handmade album, decorated at its edge with a vintage grosgrain ribbon tied in a chic 1950s bow, uses the sepia image from a postcard with its quintessential Alpine snow scene.

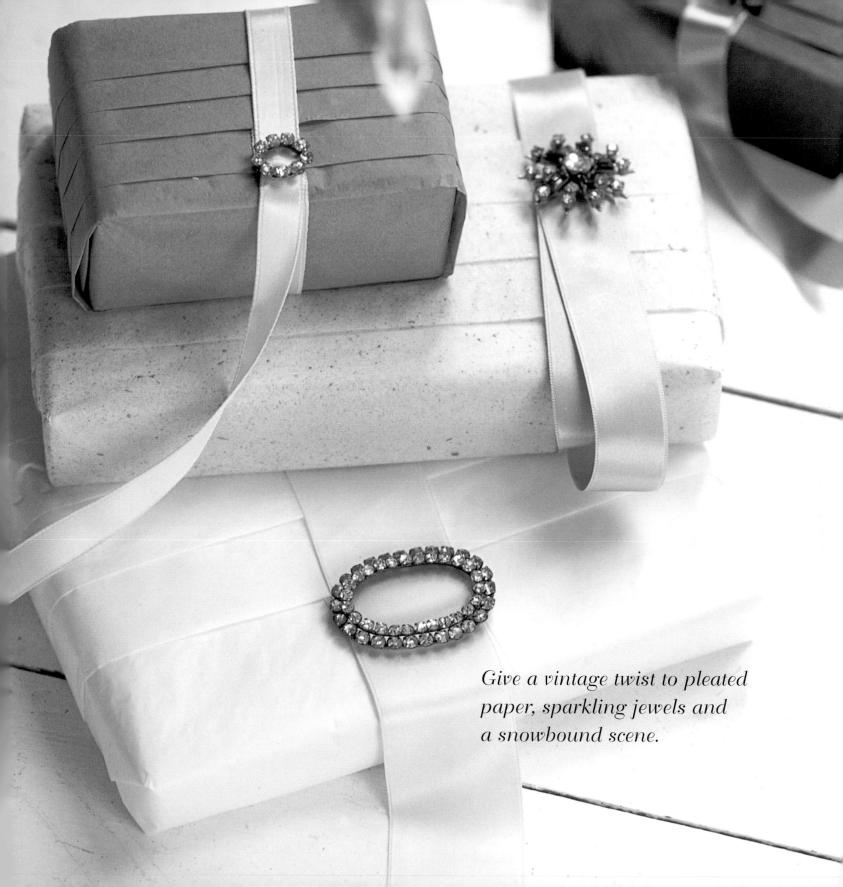

*Give a vintage twist to pleated paper, sparkling jewels and a snowbound scene.*

Old jewellery and bric-à-brac can be used to great effect when making graceful gift labels and greetings cards. Sparkling diamanté and smoky marcasite, glass and mother-of-pearl, fine silver chains and filigree – these are all perfect ingredients for making ethereal vintage tableaux. Exuding a simple compelling charm, old trinkets, buckles, buttons and clasps can be picked up for next to nothing in junk shops, market stalls or collectors' fairs. When a thoughtful selection is placed on a sheet of ivory or pure white watercolour paper, they take on an air of sophistication. Natural materials also work well. A little bundle of fragile twigs bound with gold or silver Indian wire bullion, with the addition of a single diamanté stone and a handwritten tag (again placed on a sheet of watercolour paper), makes a beautiful card or a place card at the table. They are a joy to receive, and worth treasuring long afterwards.

**This page** Fragile twigs bound with wire bullion, each with a slender handwritten tag, are glued to small cards made from watercolour paper. A single diamanté stone adds a sparkling focal point.

**Opposite right** Panelled cards made from watercolour paper display a trio of sparkling finds. Silver chains encircle the folded spines, and each card has a tissue-paper insert.

**Details opposite, top to bottom** A diamanté buckle with a scrap of ribbon; a marcasite earring; a knot of bullion wire; a marcasite button.

Piled up and waiting to be pulled, crackers are an important part of the magic and excitement of Christmas. Whether they hold a lovely gift or an amusing trinket, the childlike sense of anticipation is just the same. Crackers were invented by Tom Smith, a London confectioner who, in 1840, was inspired by the French style of wrapping bon-bons in coloured twists of paper. Borrowing the method for selling sugared almonds and other sweets, he had the idea of tucking paper mottoes, or 'kiss mottoes', inside the fancy coloured wrappers. Later he added strips of paper coated with a

## *Vintage imagery brings a touch of nostalgia to decorative crackers.*

tiny amount of explosive, to give the 'cracking' sound when they were pulled – hence the name. Eventually, sweets were omitted in favour of surprise gifts and paper hats, though of course the mottoes were retained.

Carry on this tradition by making your own crackers. For the decorative labels, use images photocopied from old postcards or Christmas cards. Choose cards with evocative illustrations, or photographs – tinted or sepia – which capture the spirit of Christmas. Either repeat the same image or pick different ones, and make photocopies in sepia or colour, depending on the originals. The vintage labels gain a fresh, modern look when trimmed with gold and placed on crackers of pure white crêpe paper. Another essential at Christmas is the Advent calendar, which celebrates each December day up to Christmas with a little token.

**This page and opposite** For decorative crackers, place a gift and motto inside a cardboard tube. Wrap in a length of crêpe paper. Twist each end and secure with jeweller's wire. Using gold paper cake 'ribbon', or the scalloped edges cut from doilies, add a border to each label and to the crackers' ends.

**Above left** A few fragile twigs of clematis or wisteria are bent into a wreath and sprinkled with single diamanté stones.
**Above centre** A little gold-edged card with a cut-out brown-paper Christmas tree is crowned with a diamanté 'star'.
**Above right** A dove cut from gilded paper, with pleated wings (made from a single piece of paper) slotted through its body, has a tiny bead for an eye.

**Below left** A golden spray of berries is created from vintage metal beads, mother-of-pearl leaves and fine wire.
**Below centre** A miniature cracker twisted from iridescent organza around a tiny cardboard tube carries a gleaming piece of bric-à-brac.
**Below right** A sprig of mistletoe is created from creamy pearls threaded through jeweller's wire and gold-painted leaves made from card.

**Opposite** A beautiful vintage Advent calendar is made from an artist's stretched canvas backed with foamboard and edged with gold metallic braid. Twenty-four miniature festive tokens (one for each day before Christmas) – some found, some handmade – are attached to luggage labels, which are numbered in gold and pinned to the canvas.

# Easter

**Celebrating the arrival of spring, vintage silk flowers and leaf-green ribbons from an Easter bonnet make becoming decorations for an Easter breakfast.**

An Easter celebration gets the lightest vintage touch. Floral hat trimmings from the 1930s – narcissi, lilies-of-the-valley, marguerites, daisies – encircle hand-lettered eggs in a garlanded centrepiece, and provide delicate decoration for painted eggs and a felted wool egg-cosy.

**This page** A sprig of narcissus glued to a painted egg; a silk flower cuts a dash in the hatband of an egg-cosy.

**Opposite** Symbols of spring: speckled eggs nesting in hat-veil; beribboned chocolate bars; vintage flowers decorating a centrepiece of painted eggs.

*Painted Easter eggs carry the message 'Spring', in different languages – because, in any country, spring is the season of hope and renewal.*

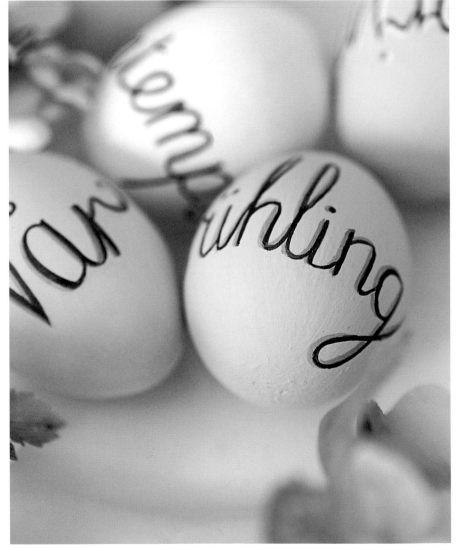

Easter has been called the Queen of Festivals, and it was considered lucky to wear a bright new piece of clothing. Traditionally, young girls and women wore a bonnet, embellished with flowers or ribbons of white, green and yellow – colours symbolic of spring. Complemented by delicate white bone china, a gentle scene is set with vintage floral hat decorations of white blossoms and green foliage, and sumptuous 1930s sateen hat ribbon. With a diluted palette of almond green, primrose, duck-egg blue and chalk white for the painted eggs, spring is at once brought into the home.

Spring denotes the season of hope and renewal, so the centrepiece with encircling blossoms of white silk flowers contains painted eggs, with the word 'Spring' hand-lettered in various languages – *Printemps, Frühling, Primavera, Spring, Vår*. Easter chocolate bars are stripped of their usual wrappings and given white paper sleeves, beautifully finished with green hat ribbons and chic paper bows – all within a table setting of silver and primrose teapots and fine bone china.

This page To prepare an egg
for painting, pierce a hole in
each end, making the hole in
the broad end larger. Blow
the contents out through the
larger hole, and rinse
through. Paint with emulsion
and, when dry, apply lettering
by hand. Sample pots of
emulsion are ideal.

Opposite left Paper sleeves,
bows and vintage ribbon give
chocolate bars a new style.

Opposite right The hand-
lettering is reminiscent of the
script iced onto traditional
Easter eggs.

# Valentines

**Romantic images and ephemera can inspire an intriguing Valentine's card, while pearls and a corsage decorate heart-shaped boxes – creating love tokens that will be remembered far beyond 14 February.**

Give in to your romantic instincts when searching for Valentine inspirations in bric-à-brac stalls. Look for illustrations of Cupid and Venus, trinkets of gold and silver, hearts lost from lockets, lovers' pins, tiny keys, delicate initials and numbers. Anything of pearl will come in useful – a bracelet or earring – and anything unexpected, such as filigree paper lace, or a rose corsage. Valentines first appeared in the fifteenth century as wood engravings. In the nineteenth century they became more sumptuous, with secret messages hidden from strict parents behind panels decorated with posies or feathers. Like their forerunners, vintage love tokens are best expressed in simple line drawings or woodcuts, and *trouvailles* discreetly presented within colours of tea and blush pink.

**Opposite above** Valentine-inspired images and ephemera decorate five rectangles cut from thin plywood or card. Cryptic messages are added using letters cut out from pamphlets or magazines. The five cards are joined together with a length of vintage ribbon, and close in a concertina fold. The ribbon ends tie in an elegant loose knot.

**Opposite below** Delicate filigree edging salvaged from a damaged Victorian card becomes the border for a piece of watercolour paper mounted on plywood. A silver heart pin and the message *Amour* complete the picture.

**This page** Heart-shaped confectionery boxes are painted in sugar-almond colours and decorated with pearls, a corsage, ribbons and silk tulle – perfect for holding small gifts or love notes.

# wedding keepsakes

Long after the day, memories are relived through keepsakes pinned to a wedding cushion and thoughts written in a guest book. So celebrate in true vintage fashion, for these tokens will be treasured for ever.

**Above and top** Pale pink and old-gold organza flowers are pinned to a velvet wedding cushion with a filigree and paste brooch; draped over the French iron daybed is a stunning beaded and embroidered vintage wedding dress.

**Right** Ivory and pink velvet bracelets for the bridesmaids are made from lengths of ribbon fastened with silk thread loops and shimmering glass buttons. A separate velvet strip holds a handmade organza bud in place on each bracelet.

On such a special day, gloriously old-fashioned colours – dusty pink, ivory, old gold, so evocative of *fin-de-siècle* romance – join together with exquisite vintage details. Wedding favours to charm your guests are decorated with vintage ribbons, buttons and beads, and will be treasured long afterwards. Silk-lined confetti boxes with luxurious bows overflow with tissue-paper petals of gold, pink and ivory. Wonderful individual flowers can be created from silk organza in old gold and pink, some in full bloom, some in bud, and all elaborated with gold wire stamens studded with tiny gold seed pearls. Slender velvet bracelets, each adorned with a single organza bud and fastened with a delicate glass button, are perfect for the bridesmaids, and become their lasting mementos of the day. Other flowers can be used for a bouquet or a corsage, or strewn over the wedding table to create a dreamy, theatrical effect, and to add to the romance of the occasion. Finally, as a tangible reminder of this momentous day, the bride takes two flowers and, with a cherished brooch, pins them to an ivory velvet wedding cushion.

**Above left** The flower petals are cut from organza, and a stem made from wire, covered with double-sided tape and bound with ribbon. The petals are folded round and glued to the stem, and the base neatened with extra organza. Stamens of jeweller's wire are decorated with pearls.

**Above right** A basic box shape is cut from card and lightly scored where necessary. The box is covered inside and out with silk, attached with spray adhesive. Once assembled, it is decorated with vintage ribbon and a silk cord handle to complete the prettiest confetti holder.

*An enchanting notebook for every guest holds sketches, photographs, messages and new friends' telephone numbers – a useful reminder of a special wedding day.*

**Above and right** For guest notebooks, small spiral-bound sketch pads are ideal. Replace the outside cover with watercolour paper. On top, paste a second sheet of paper in which a window has been cut out, and place pretty vintage buttons in the frame. Glue a paper rectangle, edged with gold, to cover the spine. A string of vintage glass beads is threaded through the spine.

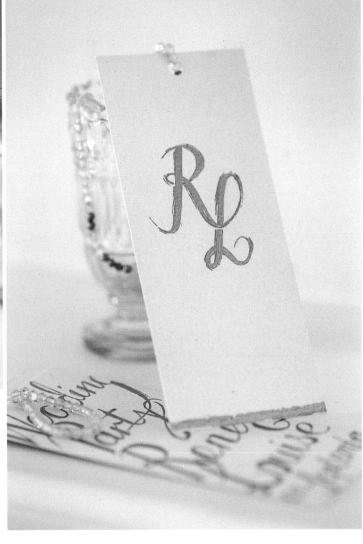

**Above** 'Sterling Silver' roses in a vase echo the old-fashioned colours of the wedding.

**Right** Invitations are made from rectangles of watercolour paper decorated at the bottom with a brushstroke of gilding paint. Use the same paint or a rollerball for the intertwined initials and, on the reverse, hand-script details of the wedding. Punch a hole at the top and thread with a string of gold and glass beads.

Weddings have a timeless quality, and the perennial beauty of vintage is utterly appropriate for the entire occasion – from the slender beaded wedding invitations hand-lettered in gold, with the entwined initials of bride and groom on one side and the wedding day details hand-scripted on the reverse, to exquisitely wrought handmade notebooks that help commemorate the day. Make a gift of a notebook to guests as they arrive, and have pens and pencils in small crystal vases so they can record their thoughts and memories, as well as the names and addresses of new friends. With each cover embellished in a subtly different way, with tiny vintage buttons and decorative handles of gold and glass beads, the notebooks will become mementos to be treasured and kept, with lasting sentimental value. Thus, with ingenuity and imagination, memorable things can be created from modest but charming ingredients.

# new baby

Pearl buttons and buckles, cream lace and silky ribbons, and a nostalgic family photograph – the perfect combination to announce the birth of a new baby.

The most wonderful announcement, the birth of a baby, can also be a touching reminder of the past, of our own childhood, and of the future. A baby announcement is a chance to use vintage items such as a favourite family photograph, a button from a christening gown, and perhaps some baby-blue ribbon found on a haberdasher's stall. Antique lace, admired throughout generations for its exquisite craftsmanship, makes lovely wrapping for a christening gift. To contrast with the texture of the lace, silky cream ribbon is tied round the gift and threaded through a tiny vintage baby buckle. Translucent sheets of glassine, normally used in photograph albums, are perfect for making large gift 'envelopes', and an excellent way to wrap a special piece of baby's clothing so that the gift can be glimpsed. Somewhere in your collection will be just the right mother-of-pearl button to sew onto the envelope with a loop of linen thread.

**Opposite** Inside an Edwardian crib is a Moses basket with a soft linen layette and a small gift wrapped in vintage lace. Over the side is a vintage embroidered net christening gown.

**Above right** A glassine envelope is decorated with a shell button and loops of linen thread. The end is left loose or wound round the button to fasten the package.

**Below right** A gift is wrapped in lace, tied with ribbon, and fastened by a delicate 1940s baby buckle.

No present is quite complete without beautiful gift wrapping, especially if the offering is a family heirloom such as a pretty, delicately hand-smocked baby dress which has been handed down from one generation to the next. The neat, pristine feel of a handmade box sets off the beauty of the gift within, while blue vintage ribbons, tied simply at each corner, give the container itself a period charm. The box is deep enough to hold several layers. Folded beneath the baby dress is a crisp linen layette and an antique lace christening gown, making a sumptuous mixture of fabrics, old and new.

For the baby announcement card, choose a special family photograph that captures a moment full of personal memories. With the addition of a fragment of vintage lace from a childhood dress at the edge, and a small pearl button tied with linen thread to fasten the card, the imagery is complete. Perhaps the card itself will one day become a treasured family heirloom.

**This page** A birth announcement is made from prints of a photograph mounted on card, and decorated with lace, thread and button, above; the envelope is made from glassine. A pile of childhood books makes a gift for a new baby, above right.

**Opposite** A gift box is made from two pieces of card, with squares cut from each corner. Fold the sides at right angles and thread ribbon through slots in each edge.

*Be inspired by precious black-and-white family photos, baby-blue ribbon and familiar children's picture books, full of memories.*

# source list

**Alfie's Antique Market**
13–25 Church Street
London NW8 8DT
Tel: 020 7723 6066
*Antique market with a comprehensive
range of stallholders*

**Annie's**
12 Camden Passage
London N1 8ED
Tel: 020 7359 0796
*Vintage clothing, accessories
and textiles*

**The Antiques Warehouse**
The Old Mill
Main Road
Marlesford, Suffolk IP13 0AG
Tel: 01728 747438
E: omtc@antiqueswarehouse.fsnet.co.uk
*Interesting antiques for the
home and garden*

**The Art Group**
146–150 Royal College Street
London NW1 0TA
Tel: 020 7428 1700
www.artgroup.com
*Colour and black-and-white cards
featuring fashion photography*

**Black Dog Antiques**
51 Earsham Street
Bungay, Suffolk NR35 1AF
Tel: 01986 895554
*General antique shop, large stock
of poster type and type cases*

**Bloomsbury Flowers**
29 Great Queen Street
London WC2B 5BB
Tel: 020 7242 2840
www.bloomsburyflowers.co.uk
*Flowers with attitude – committed to
bringing you the freshest available*

**J W Bollom**
P O Box 78
Croydon Road
Beckenham, Kent BR3 4BL
Tel: 0845 6012905
E: sales@bollom.com
*Display materials including hessian*

**Janet Bonassera**
52 Hill Rise
Richmond
Surrey TW10 6UB
Mobile: 07949 830126
*Decorative antiques for the
home and garden*

**Books and Collectables**
Unit 7/8, Railway Arches
Coldhams Road
Cambridge CB1 3EW
Tel: 01223 412845
*Second-hand books and ephemera*

**Broadwick Silks**
9–11 Broadwick Street
London W1F 0DB
Tel: 020 7734 3320
*Wide range of fabrics, specializing
in ornate and beaded silks*

**Bude Time**
Higher Wharf, Vicarage Road
Bude, Cornwall EX23 8LW
Tel: 01288 353832
E: sales@budetime.co.uk
*Specialist in quartz clock movements,
bezels, hands, dials*

**The Button Lady**
Hampstead Antique & Craft Emporium
12 Heath Street
London NW3 6TE
Tel: 020 7435 5412
Fax: 020 8440 5600
*Antique and modern buttons,
buckles and hatpins*

**The Button Queen**
19 Marylebone Lane
London W1U 2NF
Tel: 020 7935 1505
*Buttons from eighteenth century
to modern day*

**Camden Passage Market (Wed, Sat)**
Pierrepont Row
London N1 8EE
Enquiries: 020 7359 0796
*Wide variety of antiques, textiles,
jewellery, bric-à-brac*

**The Cloth House**
98 Berwick Street
London W1F 0QJ
Tel: 020 7287 1555
*A range of unusual modern fabrics
including lycra and polyester 'paper'*

**Cloud Cuckoo Land**
6 Charlton Place
London N1 8AJ
Tel: 020 7354 3141
E. cuckoolandmail@yahoo.co.uk
www.cloudcuckooland.org.uk
*Vintage clothing and accessories
(1880–1970)*

**Rosemary Conquest Antiques**
4 Charlton Place
London N1 8AJ
Tel: 020 7359 0616
E: rosemary@rosemaryconquest.com
*Antiques, chandeliers and objets d'art*

**Create the Mood Publications**
Redcote, 228 Sydenham Road
Croydon, Surrey CR0 2EB
E: thegarter@createthemood.uklinux.net
*Publishers of The Garter – the
directory that supports costuming*

**Creative Beadcraft**
20 Beak Street
London W1F 9RE
Tel: 020 7629 9964
Mail order tel: 01494 715606
www.creativebeadcraft.co.uk
*Beads, sequins, feathers, jeweller's wire*

**Curtis Fine Papers**
Main Street
Guardbridge
St Andrews
Fife KY16 0UU
Tel: 01334 839551
www.curtisfinepapers.com
*Speciality papers, by mail order.*

**Designers Guild Home Store**
261–271 King's Road
London SW3 5EN
Tel: 020 7351 5775
www.designersguild.com
*Unique home products and fabrics*

**The Dining Room Shop**
62–64 White Hart Lane
London SW13 0PZ
Tel: 020 8878 1020
www.thediningroomshop.co.uk
*Antique dining furniture, glass,
china, cutlery, table linen and
furniture made to order*

**Eclectica**
2 Charlton Place
London N1 8AJ
Tel: 020 7226 5625
E. eclecticaliz@yahoo.co.uk
*Vintage costume jewellery and
contemporary designer jewellery*

**Elveden Farms, Estate Office**
Elveden, Thetford
Norfolk IP24 3TQ
Tel: 01842 890223
*Growers of premium quality Christmas
trees for internal and external displays*

**The Fisher Hall Antiques
and Collectors Fair**
Guildhall Place
Cambridge CB2 3NH
Enquiries: 01933 386986 for dates
*Wide variety of stalls: vintage jewellery,
sewing paraphernalia, table linens*

**Christina Friel**
Cambridge Sunday Arts, Craft and
Antiques Market
Pitch DL, Guildhall Square
Cambridge CB2 3QJ
E: alex.christina@virgin.net
*Vintage scarves and accessories,
fashion and accessory designer*

**Focus Gallery**
43 Museum Street
London WC1A 1LY
Tel: 020 7242 7191
*Photography gallery, fine
photographic prints*

**Friend or Faux**
28 Earsham Street
Bungay
Suffolk NR35 IAQ
Tel: 01986 896170
*Decorative antiques, porcelain, lighting,
furniture and specialist paint finishes*

**The Getty Images Gallery**
3 Jubilee Place
London SW3 3TD
Tel: 020 7376 4525
www.gettyimages.com
*Unique, affordable editions of
hand-printed photographs*

**Granta Coins, Stamps & Antiquities**
23 Magdalene Street
Cambridge CB3 0AF
Tel: 01223 361662
www.grantacoins.golinq.com
*Coins, stamps, picture postcards,
banknotes, militaria*

**Judy Greenwood Antiques**
657 Fulham Road
London SW6 5PY
Tel: 020 7736 6037
*French decorative antiques
and lighting*

**Janis Hancock**
Tel: 01933 386986
Mobile: 07702 885403
*Vintage jewellery specialist*

**Kate Hanlon**
Tel: 01799 500510
E: kate.hanlon@ntlworld.com
*Period costume and accessories*

**The Haunted Bookshop**
9 St Edward's Passage
Cambridge CB2 3PJ
Tel: 01223 312913
E: sarahkey@hauntedbooks.demon.co.uk
*Children's and illustrated books*

**Heffers Art & Graphics**
15 King Street
Cambridge CB1 ILH
Tel: 01223 568495
www.heffers.co.uk
*All art materials*

**The Hive**
Unit 3, Dales Brewery
Gwydir Street
Cambridge CB1 2LG
Tel: 01223 300269
*Antiques, bric-à-brac, vintage
jewellery and clothing*

**Hobby Stores**
40 High Street
Trumpington, Cambridge CB2 2LS
Tel: 01223 845477
E: mark_brown@HobbyStores.co.uk
*Craft materials, glues, balsa and
plywood (other stores in UK)*

**Lankester Antiques & Books**
The Old Sun Inn
29 Church Street
Saffron Walden
Essex CB10 1JW
Tel: 01799 522685
*Antiques, books, music manuscripts*

**Sarah Lewis and June Victor**
SO 40–43, Alfie's Antique Market
13–25 Church Street
London NW8 8DT
Tel: 020 7723 6105
*Vintage textiles and clothing, trimmings,
cushions, decorative objects*

**The Long Room**
111 Sheen Lane
London SW14 8AE
Tel: 020 8392 4966
*French and English decorative antiques*

**MacCulloch & Wallis**
25–26 Dering Street
London W1S 1AT
Tel: 020 7629 0311
www.macculloch-wallis.co.uk
*Fabrics, haberdashery and millinery*

**Andrew Martin**
200 Walton Street
London SW3 2JL
Tel: 020 7225 5100
*Modern and antique fabrics,
furniture and accessories*

**The Natural Fabric Company**
Wessex Place
127 High Street
Hungerford
Berks RG17 0DL
Tel: 01488 684002
*Checks, plains and stripes in cottons
and linens. Mail order available*

**Peggies Pandora**
10 Cross Keys Mews
Market Square
St Neots
Cambridgeshire PE19 2AR
Tel: 01480 403580
*Picture postcards*

**Prêt à Vivre**
Tel: 0845 1305161
www.pretavivre.com
*By mail order: silks and other fabrics,
made to measure curtains and blinds*

**V V Rouleaux**
6 Marylebone High Street
London W1U 4NJ
Tel: 020 7224 5179

also at 54 Cliveden Place
London SW1W 8AX
Tel: 020 7730 3125
www.vvrouleaux.com
*Ribbons, trimming, braid,*
*couture flowers*

**Russell & Chapple**
68 Drury Lane
London WC2B 5SP
Tel: 020 7836 7521
www.RandC.net
*Canvas, hessian and art materials*

**Josephine Ryan Antiques**
63 Abbeville Road
London SW4 9JW
Tel/Fax: 020 8675 3900
*Antiques, interiors, painted furniture,*
*armchairs, glassware, chandeliers*

**Saffron Walden Antiques Centre**
1 Market Row
Saffron Walden
Essex CB10 1HA
Tel: 01799 524534
*Antiques, collectables and bygones*

**Sandra Jane**
46–48 King Street
Cambridge CB1 1LN
Tel: 01223 323211
www.sandrajane.co.uk
*Stockists of Lewis and Wood light*
*linen canvas, furniture, fabrics and*
*home accessories*

**School Farm Antiques**
30 Earsham Street
Bungay, Suffolk NR35 1AQ
Tel: 01986 781640
*Kitchen and dairy furniture,*
*accessories and artefacts*

**T Schotte Antiques**
The Old Bakehouse
Blackmill Road
Southwold IP18 6AQ
Tel: 01502 722083
*Small but interesting range of antiques*

**Silvan Ltd**
Tel: 020 8950 8160
E: silvanltd@aol.com
*Mail order: contemporary lace, net,*
*trimmings, cotton and silk tulle*

**Soho Silks**
22 D'Arblay Street
London W1F 8EG
Tel: 020 7434 3306
*A wide range of fabrics*

**Steinberg & Tolkien**
193 Kings Road
London SW3 5EB
Tel: 020 7376 3660
*Vintage clothing, costume jewellery*
*and accessories*

**Vintage Style**
E: jane@vintagestyle.co.uk
*Commissions for any projects in this*
*book: Jane Cassini*

**Volga Linen Company**
Unit 1D Eastlands Road Industrial Estate
Leiston, Suffolk 1P16 4LL
Tel: 01728 635020 for mail order
www.volgalinen.co.uk
*Moses baskets, pram baby sets, bed and*
*table linen, day and night wear, curtains*
*and accessories, all of finest quality flax*

**Jessica Ward**
Tel: 020 7278 5058
*Decorative antiques*

**Josiah Wedgwood & Sons**
Barlaston, Stoke-on-Trent
Staffordshire ST12 9ES
Tel: 01782 204141
www.wedgwood.com
*Fine bone china and earthenware*

# picture credits

The publisher would like to thank the following
for items used in photographing this book and/or
allowing us to photograph their shops:
Annie's, The Button Lady, Cloud Cuckoo Land,
Rosemary Conquest and Eclectica.

In addition, the authors and publisher would like
to thank the owners of Fife House in Kemptown,
Brighton for allowing us to photograph their home.

# index

# acknowledgments

**Thank you to:**
Caroline Arber for her beautiful photography and creativity, and to her assistants Ciaran Oliver, Josh Kearns, Etienne Roberts.

Alison Starling who saw the potential in the project and made it possible, and everyone at Ryland Peters and Small especially Sally Powell and Clare Double.

Maggie Roberts for her valuable contributions to the text; Martin Cassini for his vital contributions to the text and copy editing; Joyce Evans for her exquisite sewing.

All the stallholders and shop owners who were so helpful.

Cathy Madoc Jones, John MacLachlan and Kathie Conn for the use of vintage items from their private collections; Baśka Dunaj for the hatboxes; Merry Brownfield for her print *Model Backstage*.

**For their kind permission to use the following extracts:**
*The Glass of Fashion* by Cecil Beaton: Extracts published by kind permission of The Literary Trustees of Sir Cecil Beaton, Rupert Crew Limited and Weidenfeld & Nicolson.
*Encyclopedia of Needlework* by Thérèse de Dillmont. DMC Library, Paris.
*The Big Book of Needlecraft* edited by Annie S. Paterson. Odhams Press.

The authors have made every effort to secure permission for works in copyright. The publisher will be happy to amend any errors or omissions in future editions.

**The following images are courtesy of:**
Dorothy Bohm: *Lisbon*, 1954.
Thurston Hopkins: *Couple at party*, 1955. The Getty Images Gallery.
Norman Parkinson: *Pamela Minchin, Jump*, 1939. Norman Parkinson Ltd and Fiona Cowan.
p.72 Donald Silverstein © Vogue, The Condé Nast Publications Ltd.
Chris Ware: *Elizabeth Taylor feeds the pigeons in Trafalgar Square*, 1950. Keystone Collection, The Getty Images Gallery.
*Gary Cooper and family on bicycles*, Maria Cooper Janis, c/o The Lantz Office, New York, USA.

**On a personal note:**
A special thankyou to all the friends who helped, especially during the school holidays and while I was on the photographic shoot. Thank you to Martin for everything, to my mother, Joyce, who inspired me, and to my wonderful son, Roman, for his effervescence and good humour throughout.
**Jane Cassini**

A big 'thank you' to my husband, Mick, for his constant love and support, and to Pep, who missed her long walks.
**Ann Brownfield**